Cats Coloring Book For Adults

GIANT CATS

Fantasy Art Coloring Book For Stress Relief

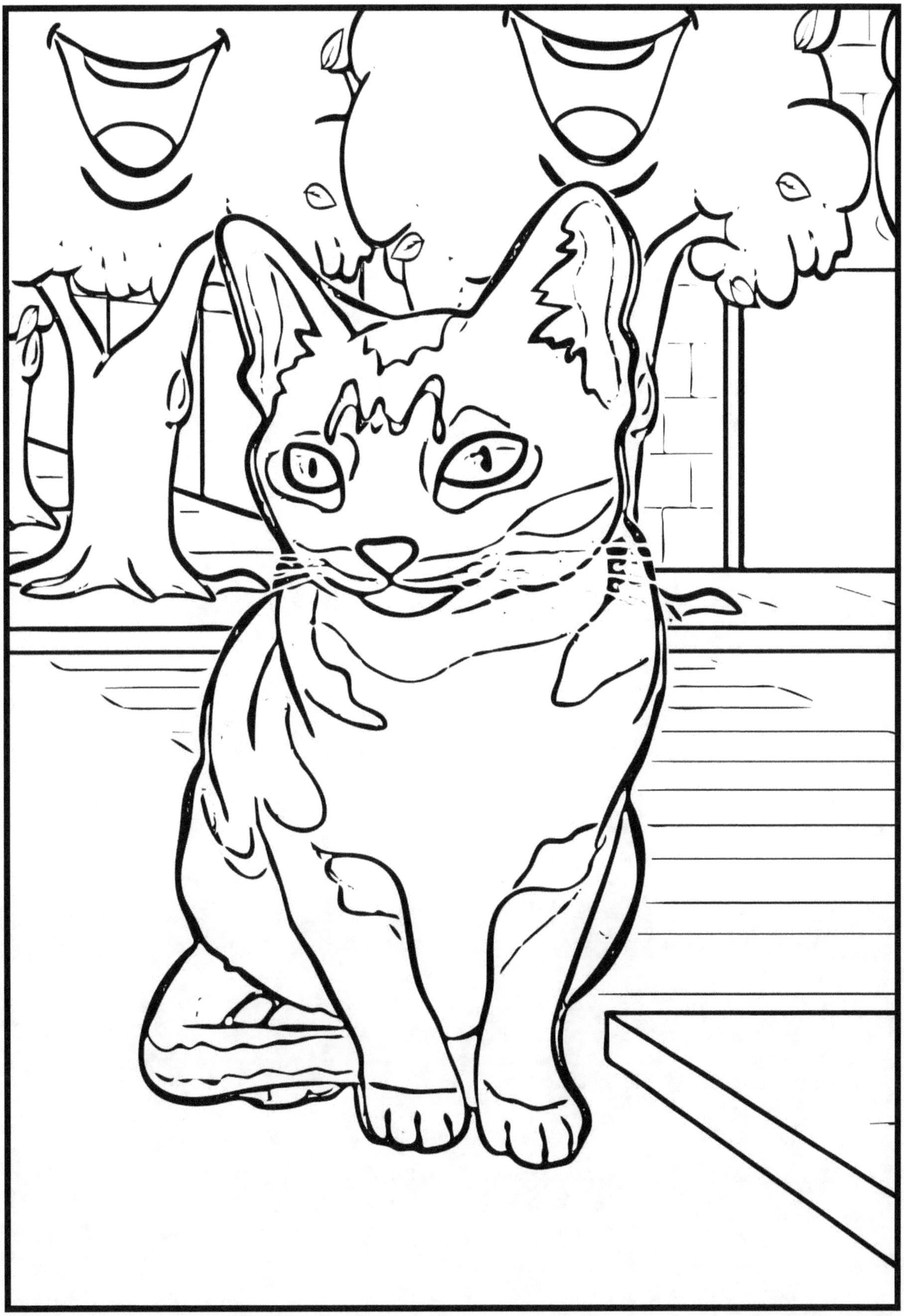

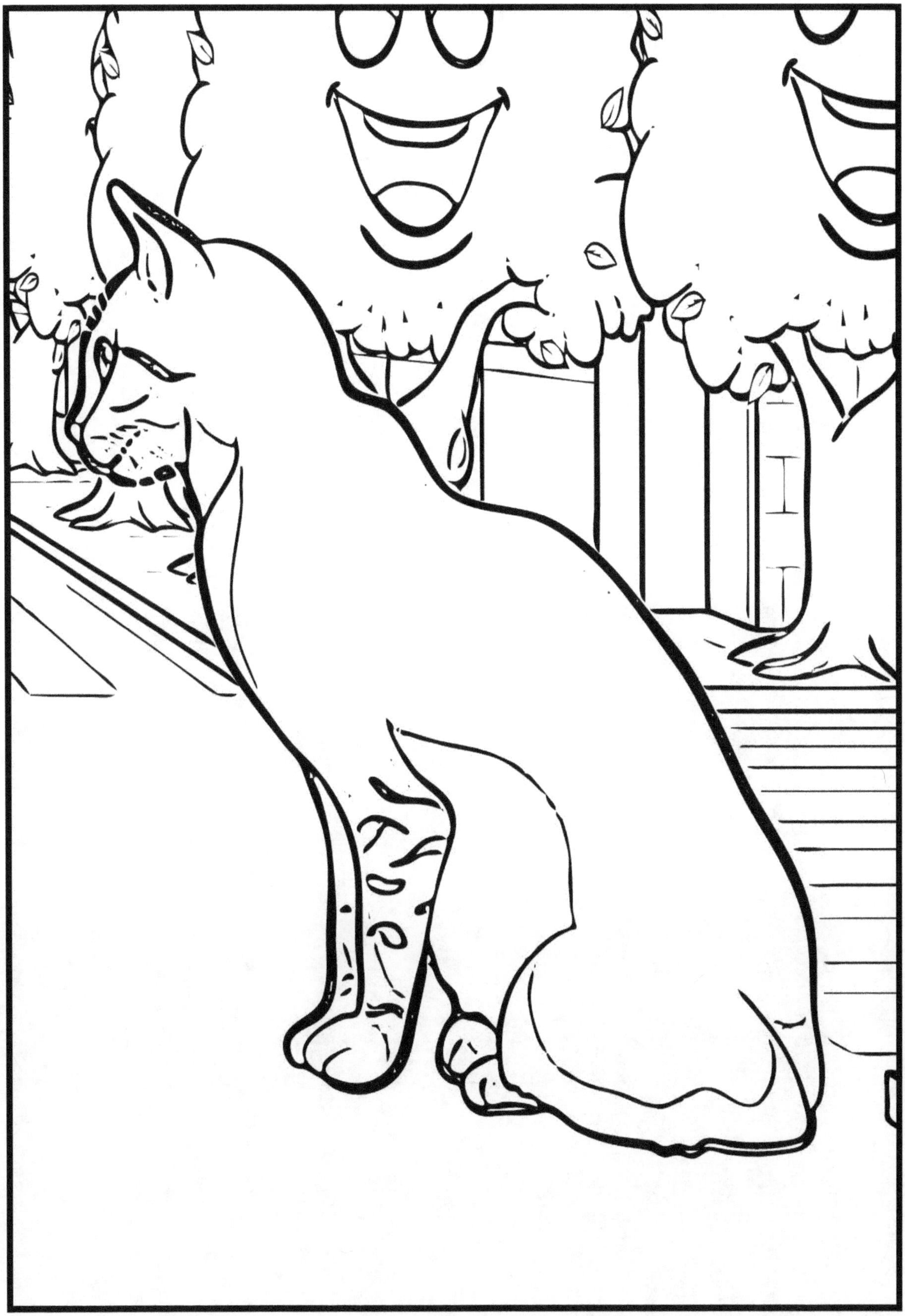

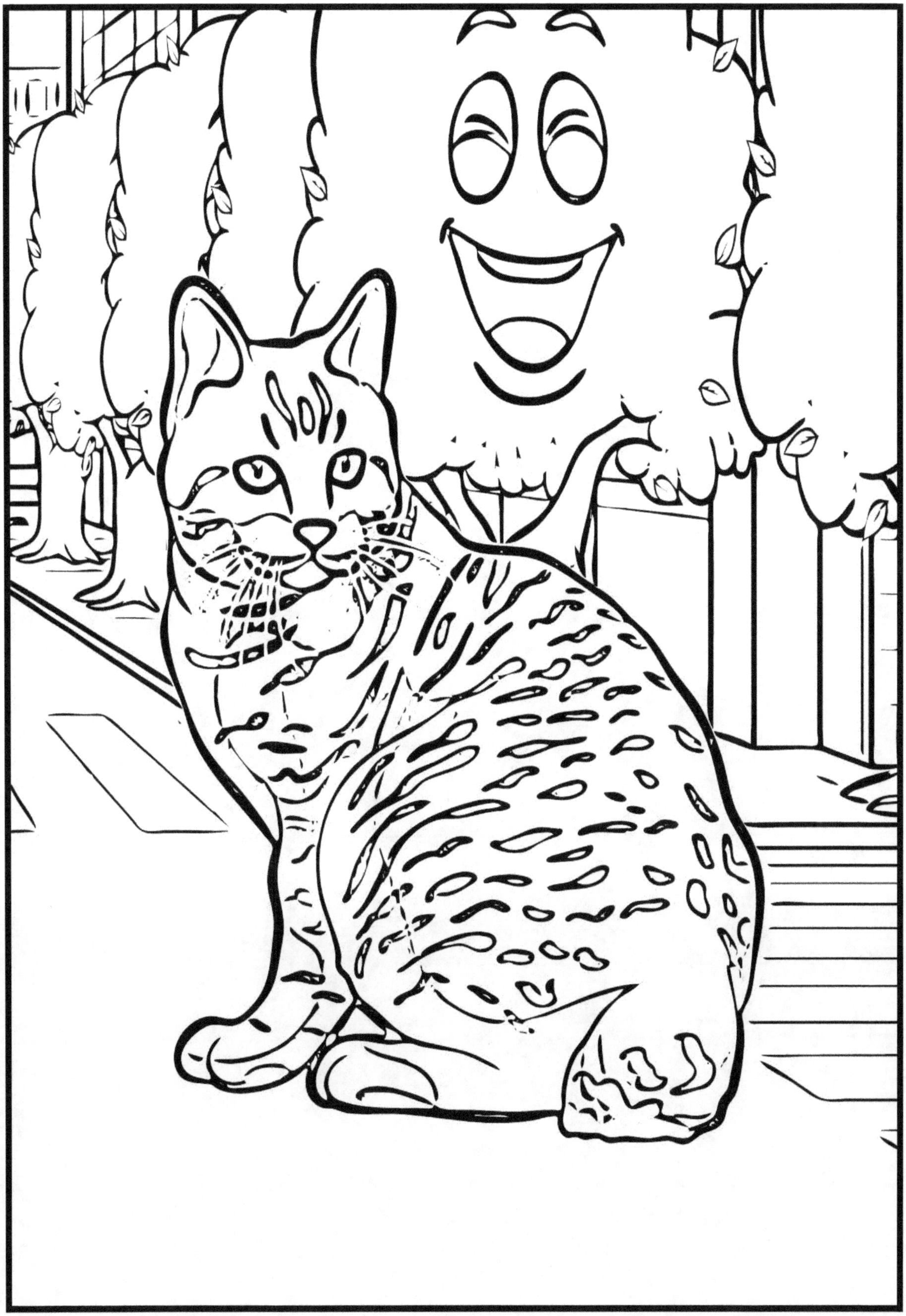

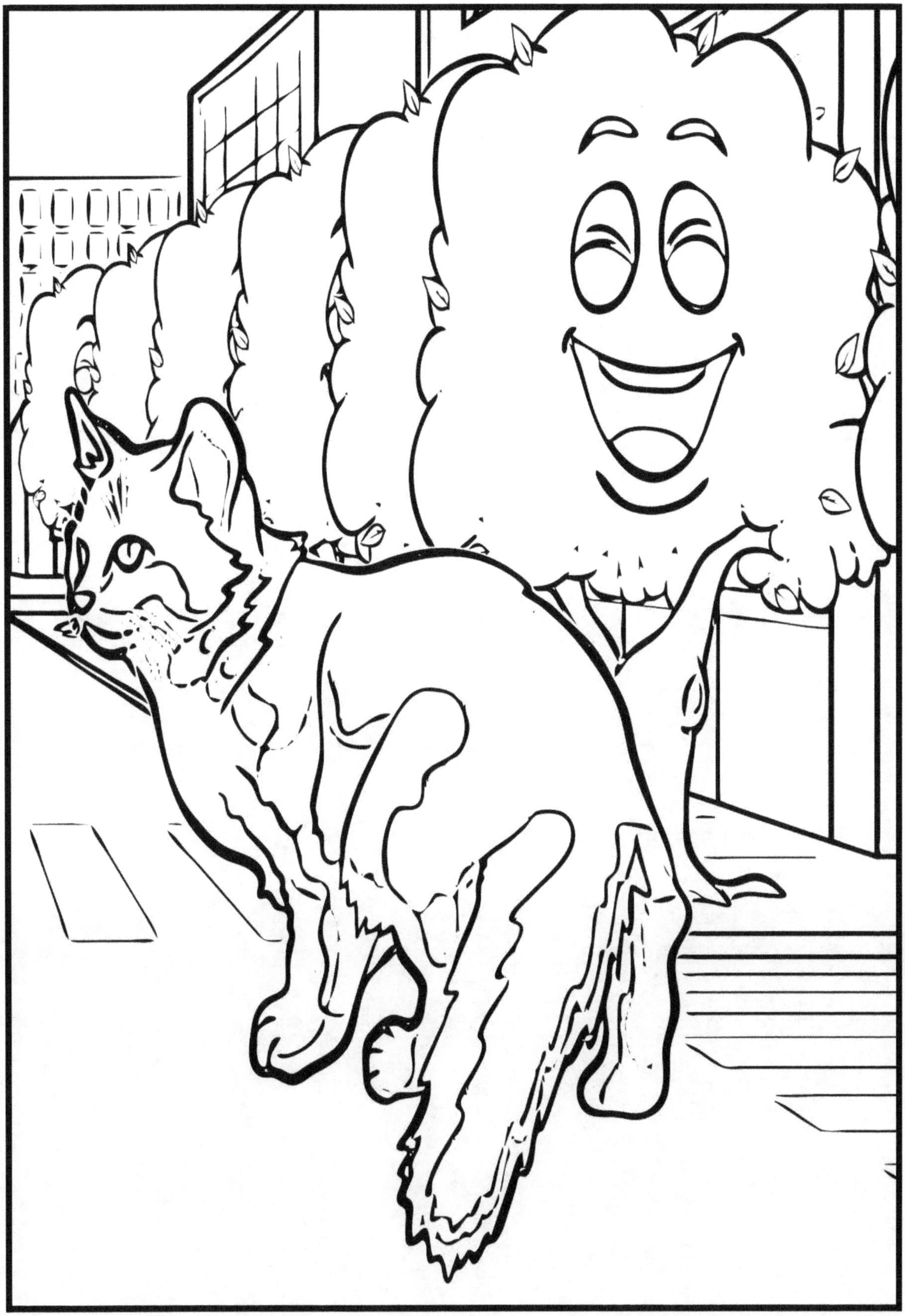

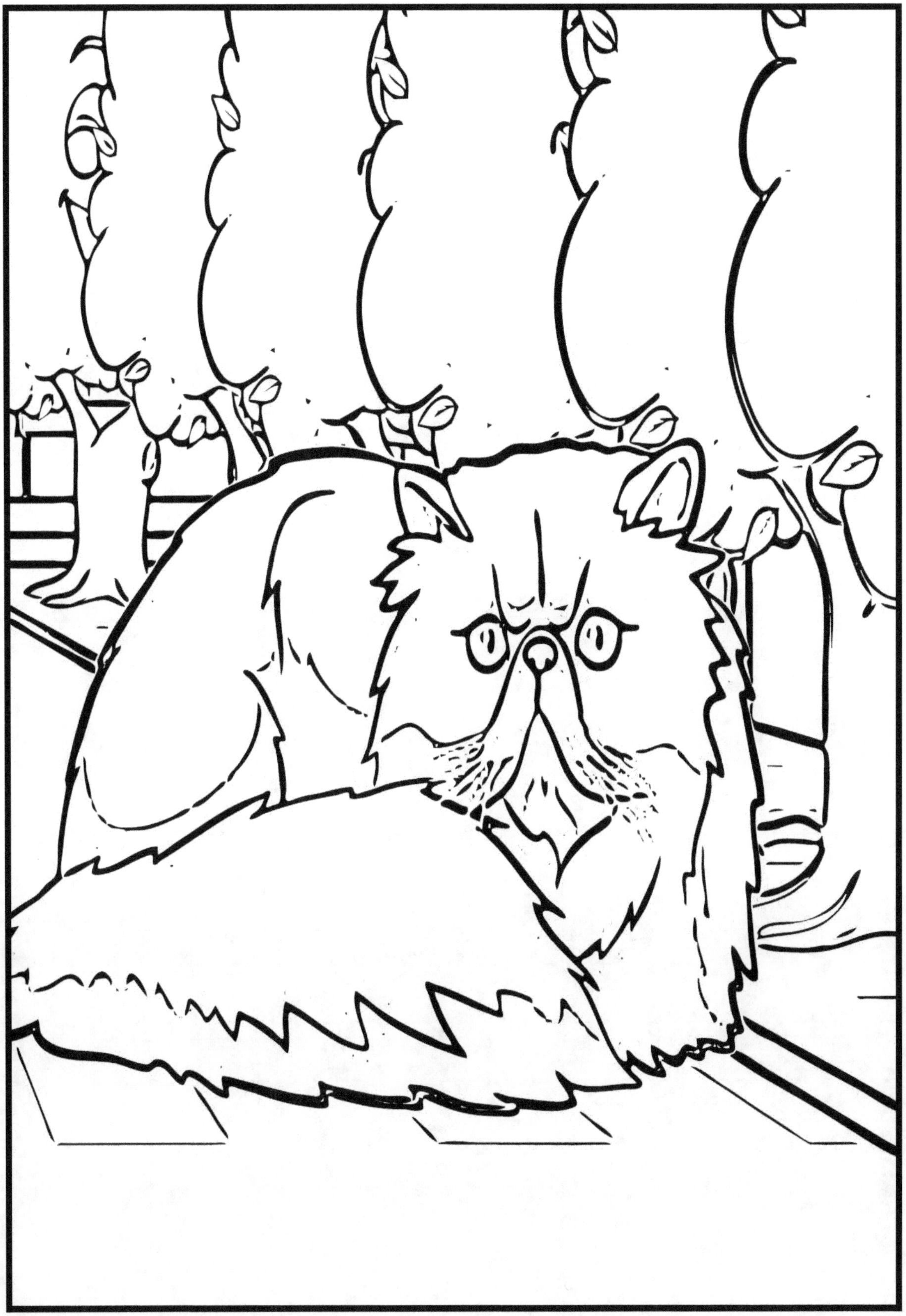

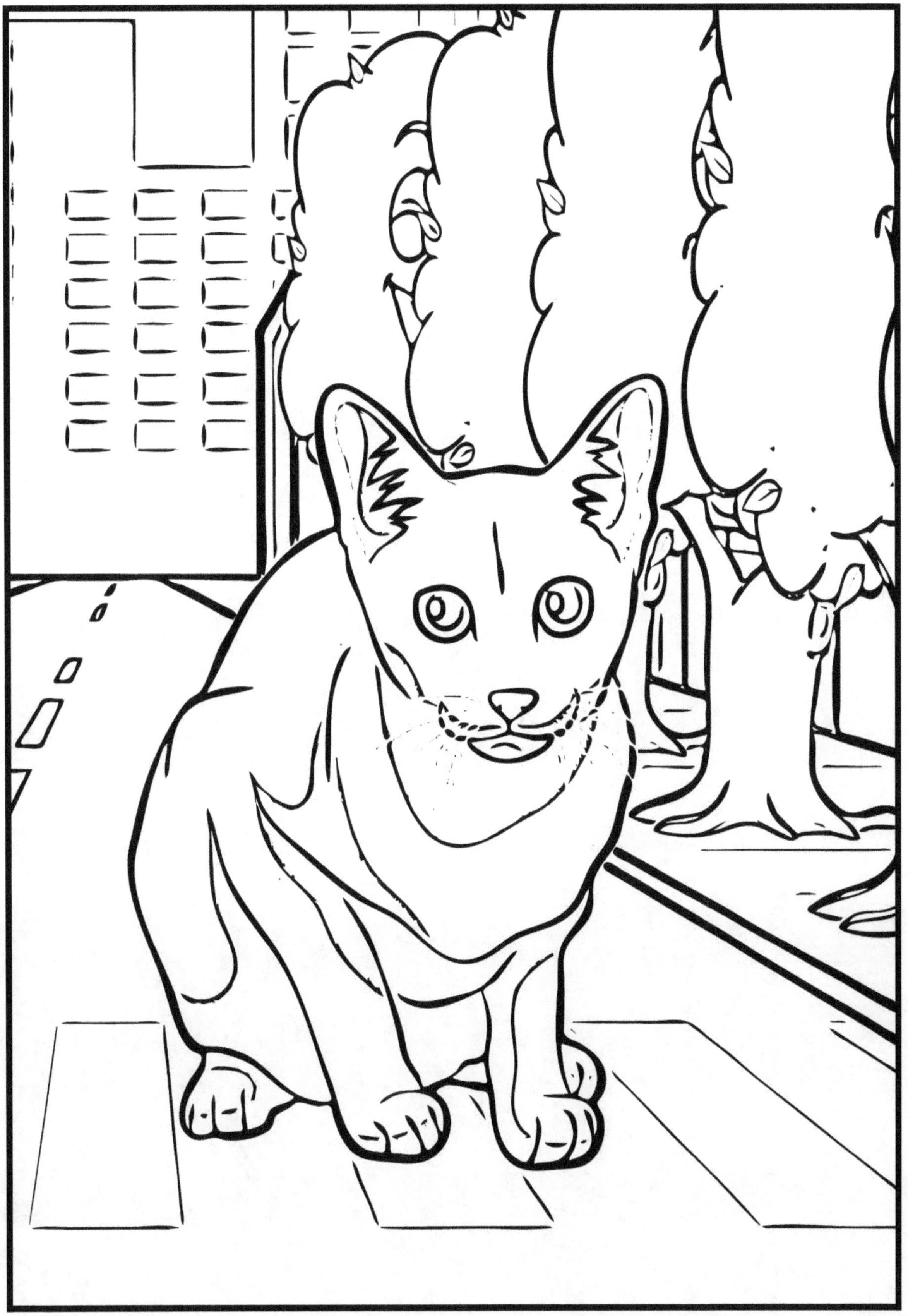

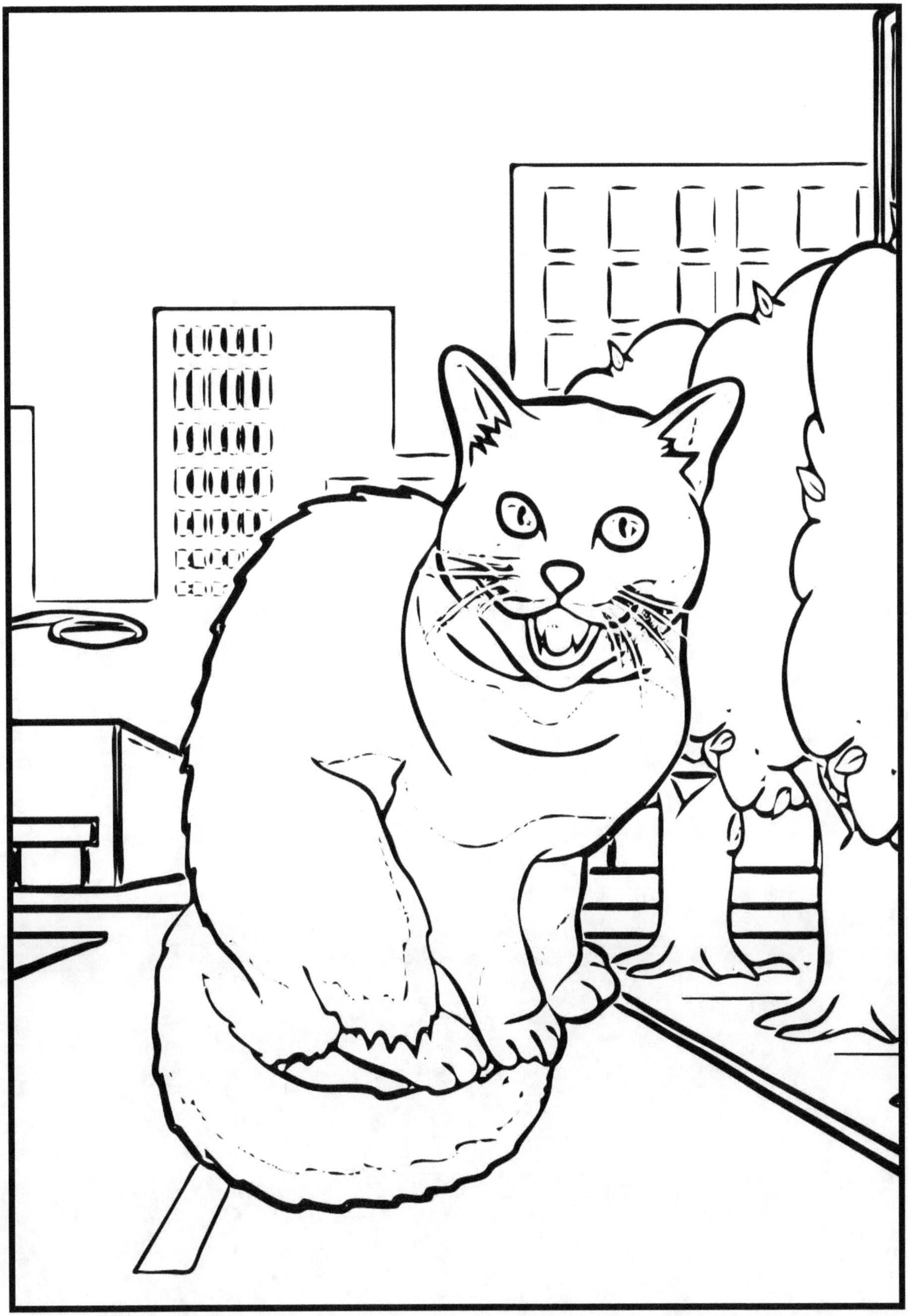

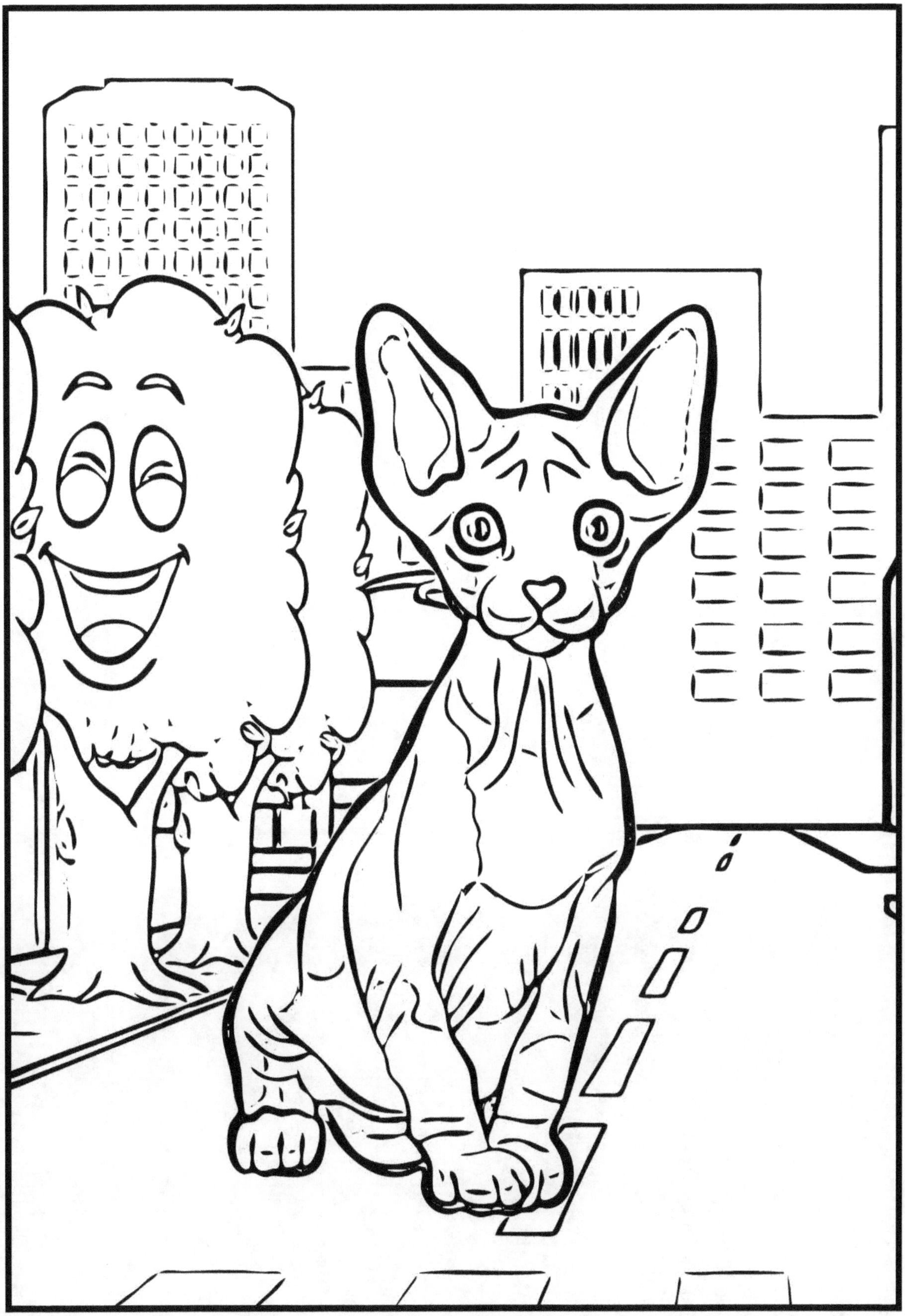

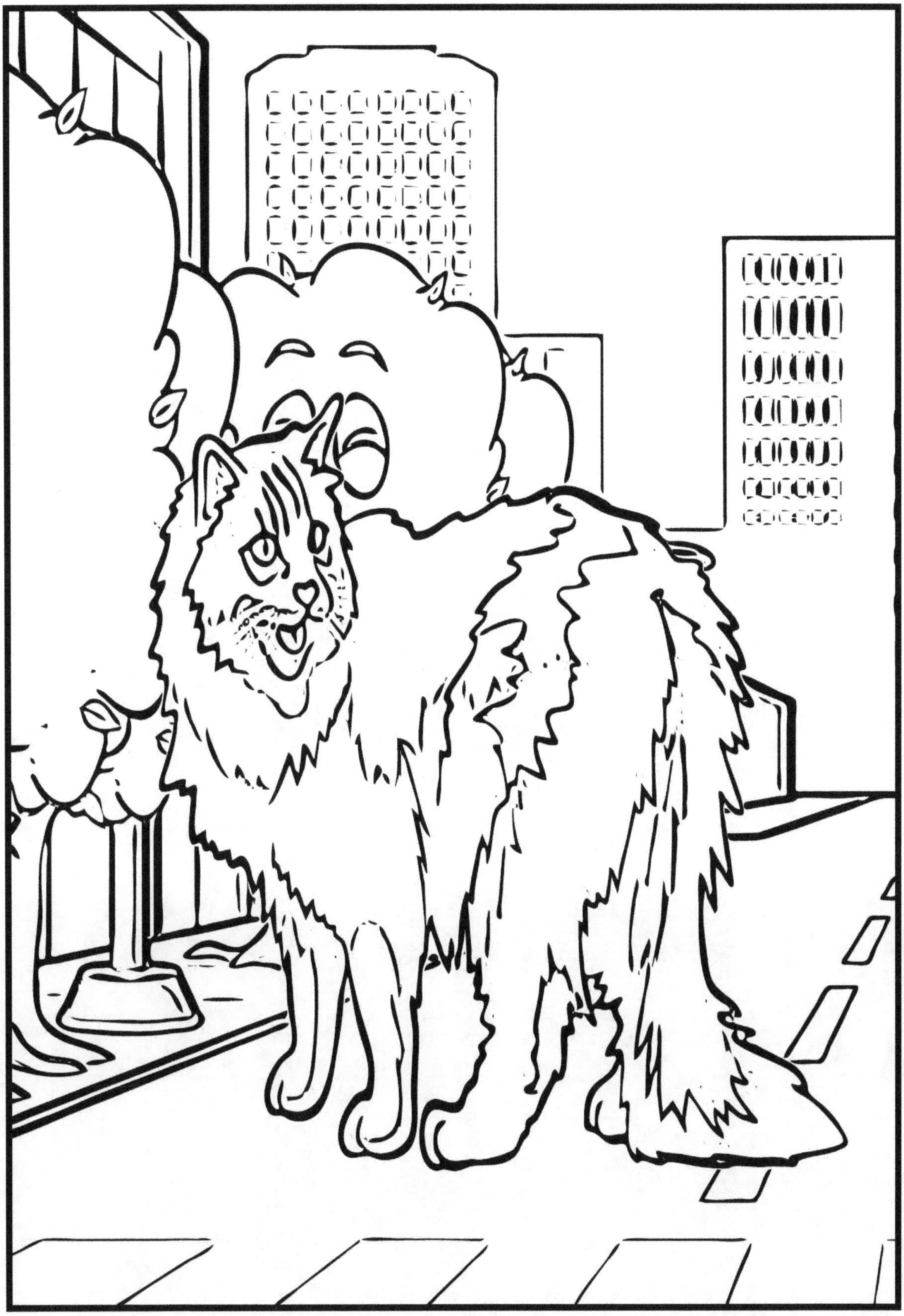

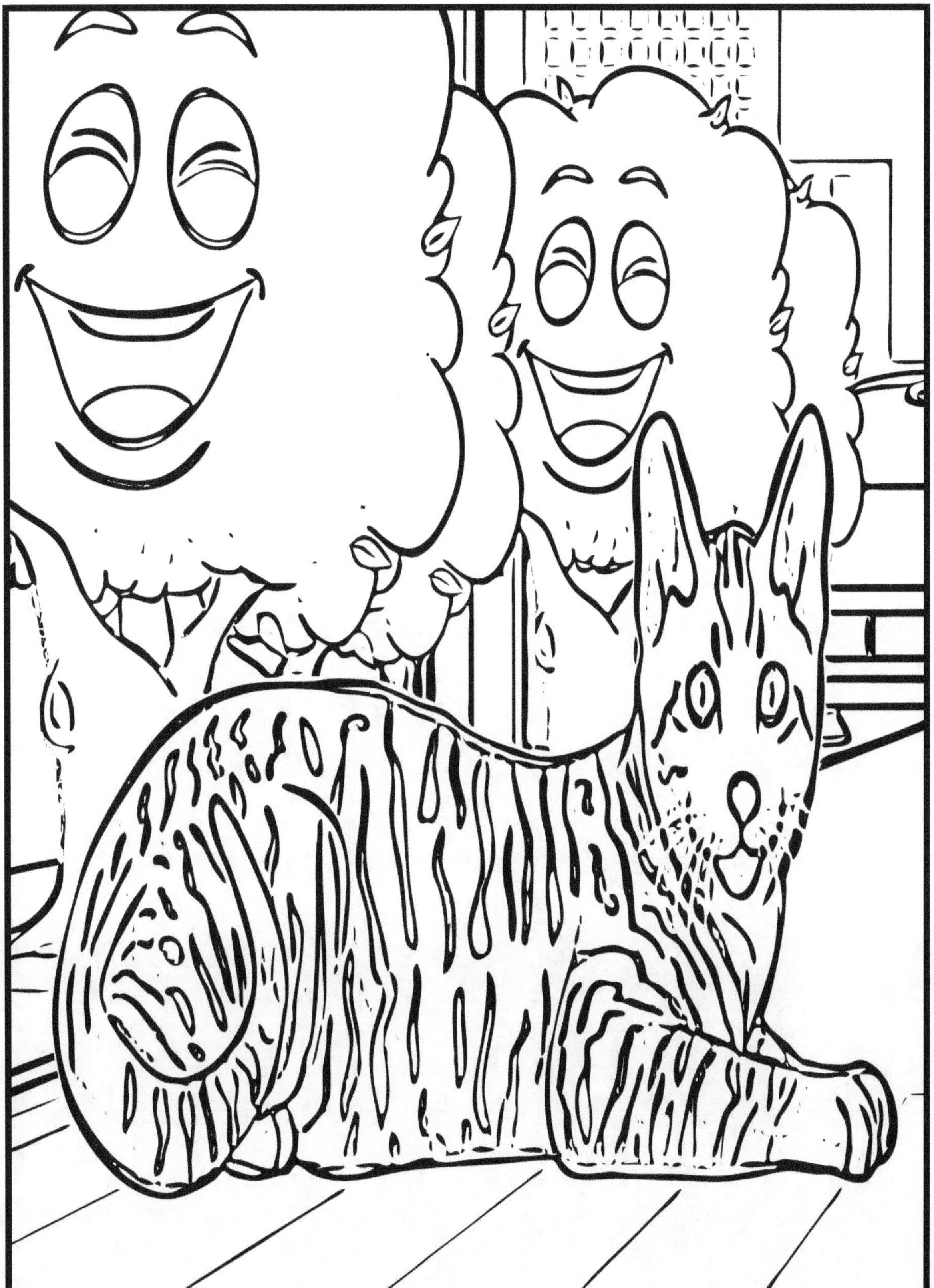

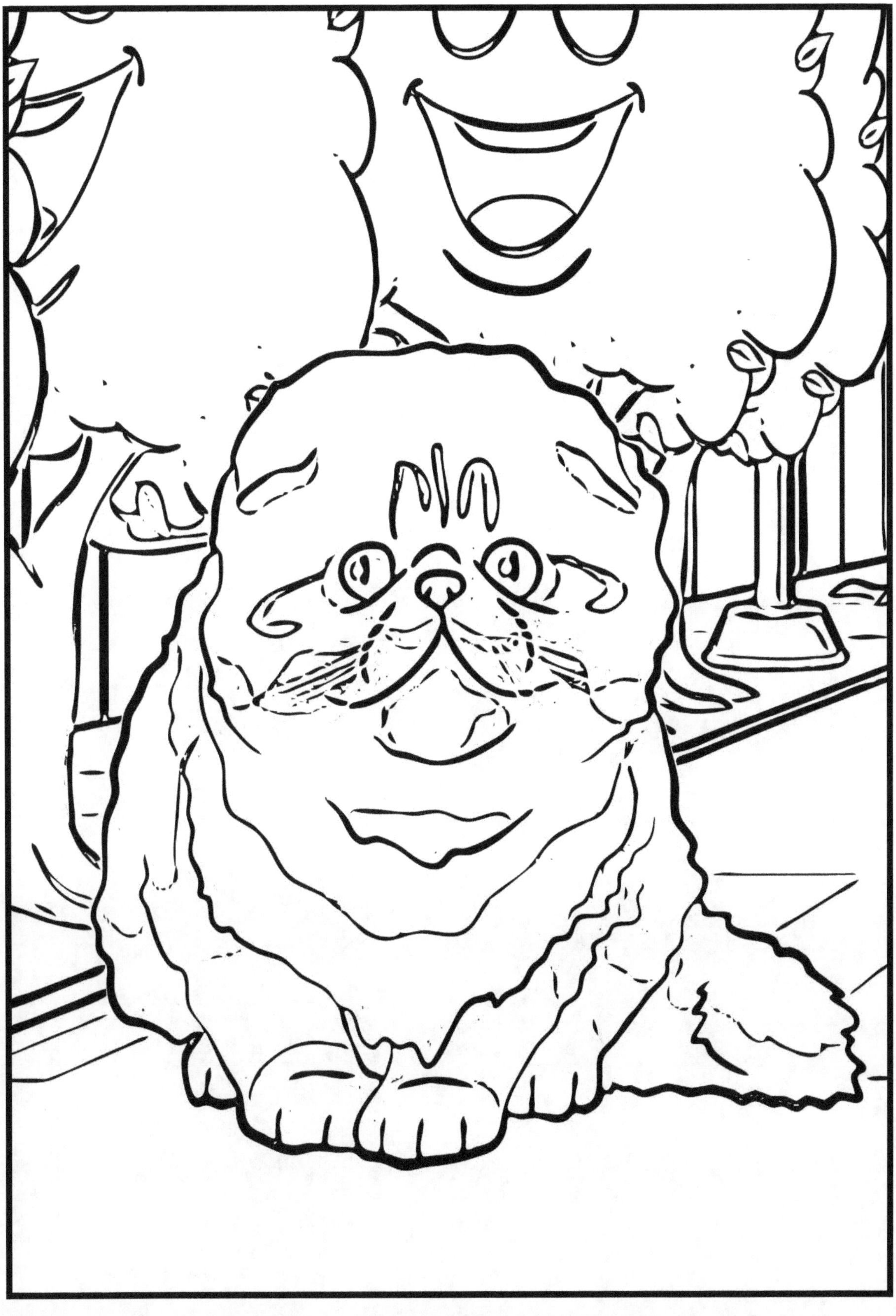

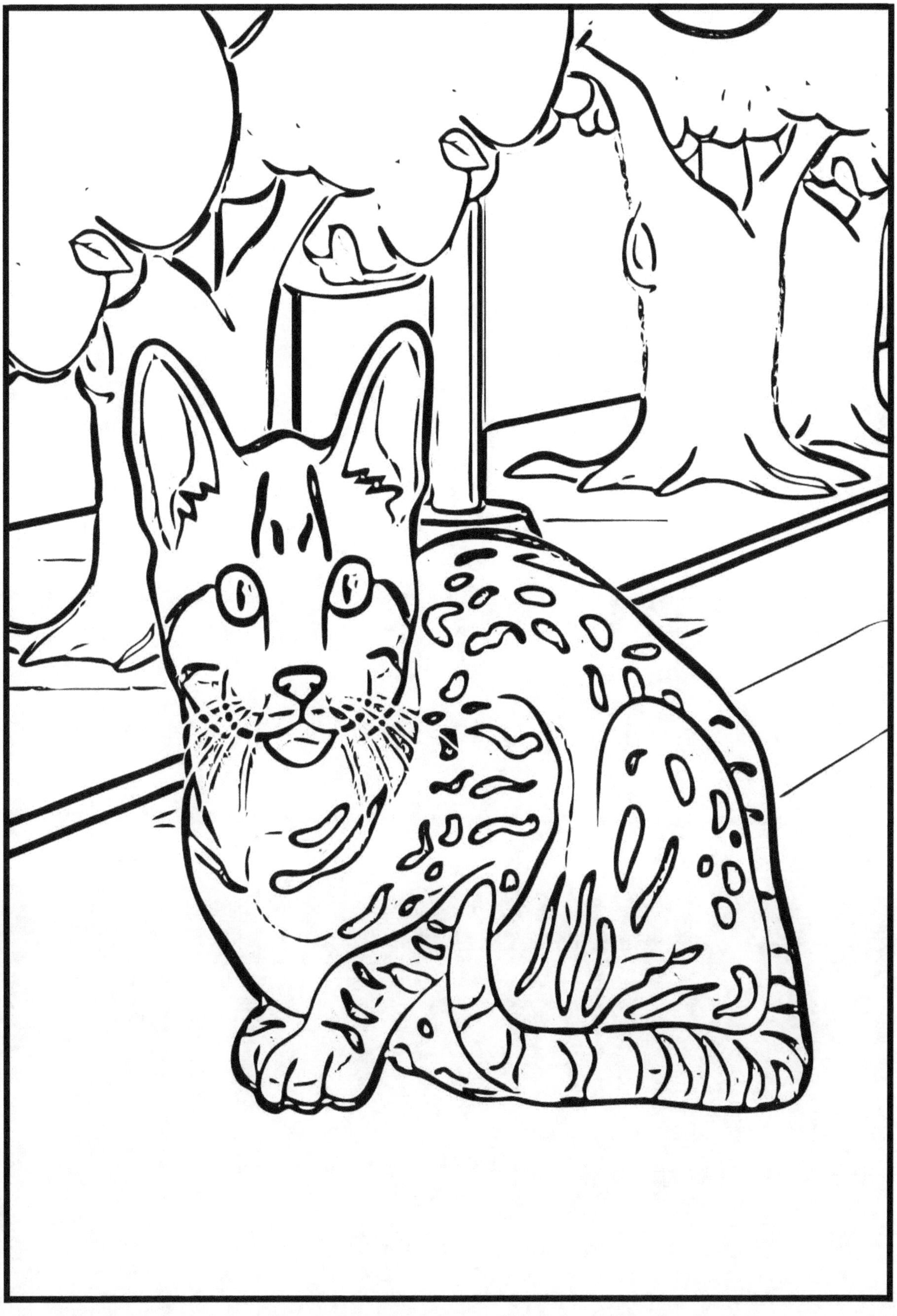

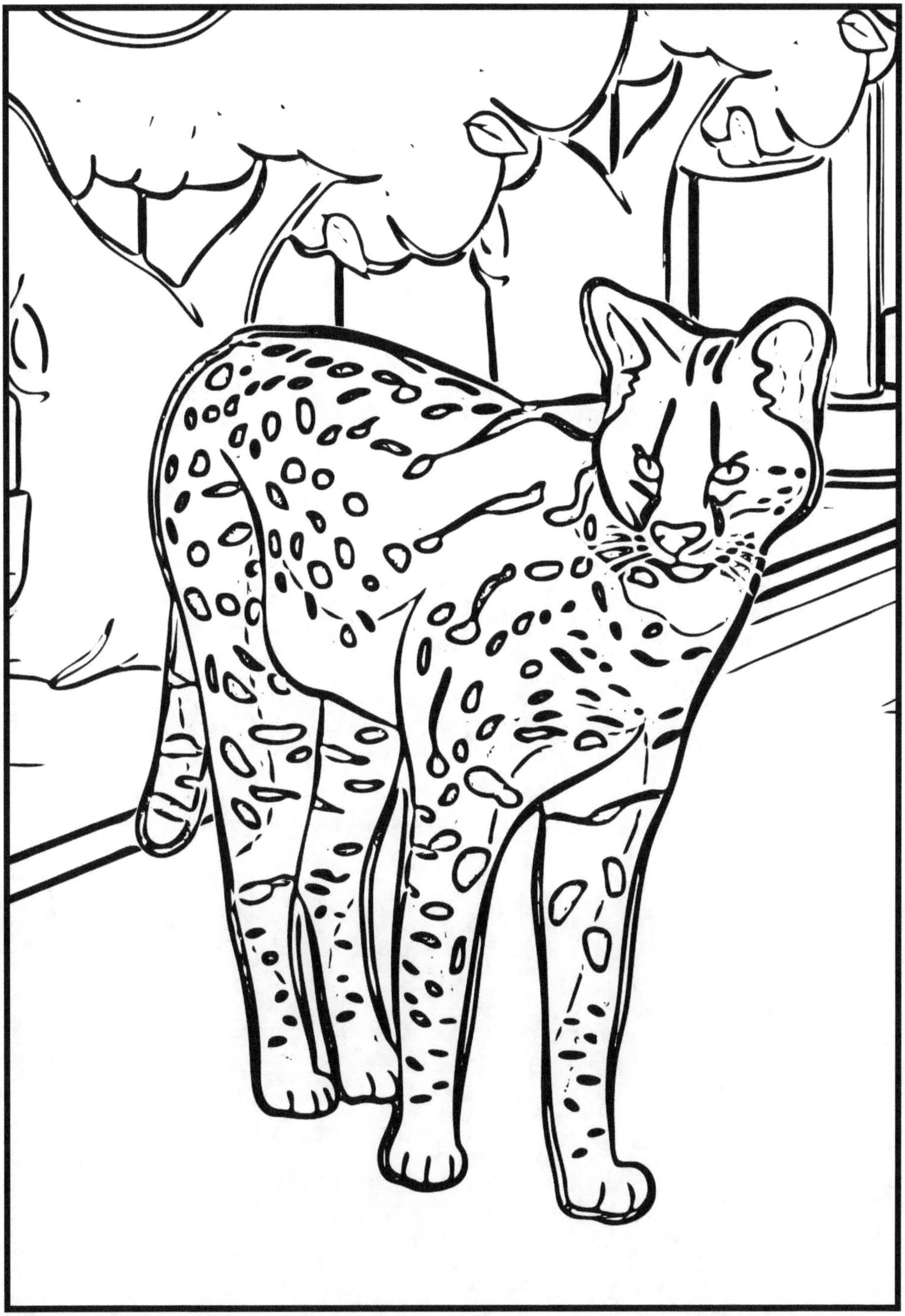

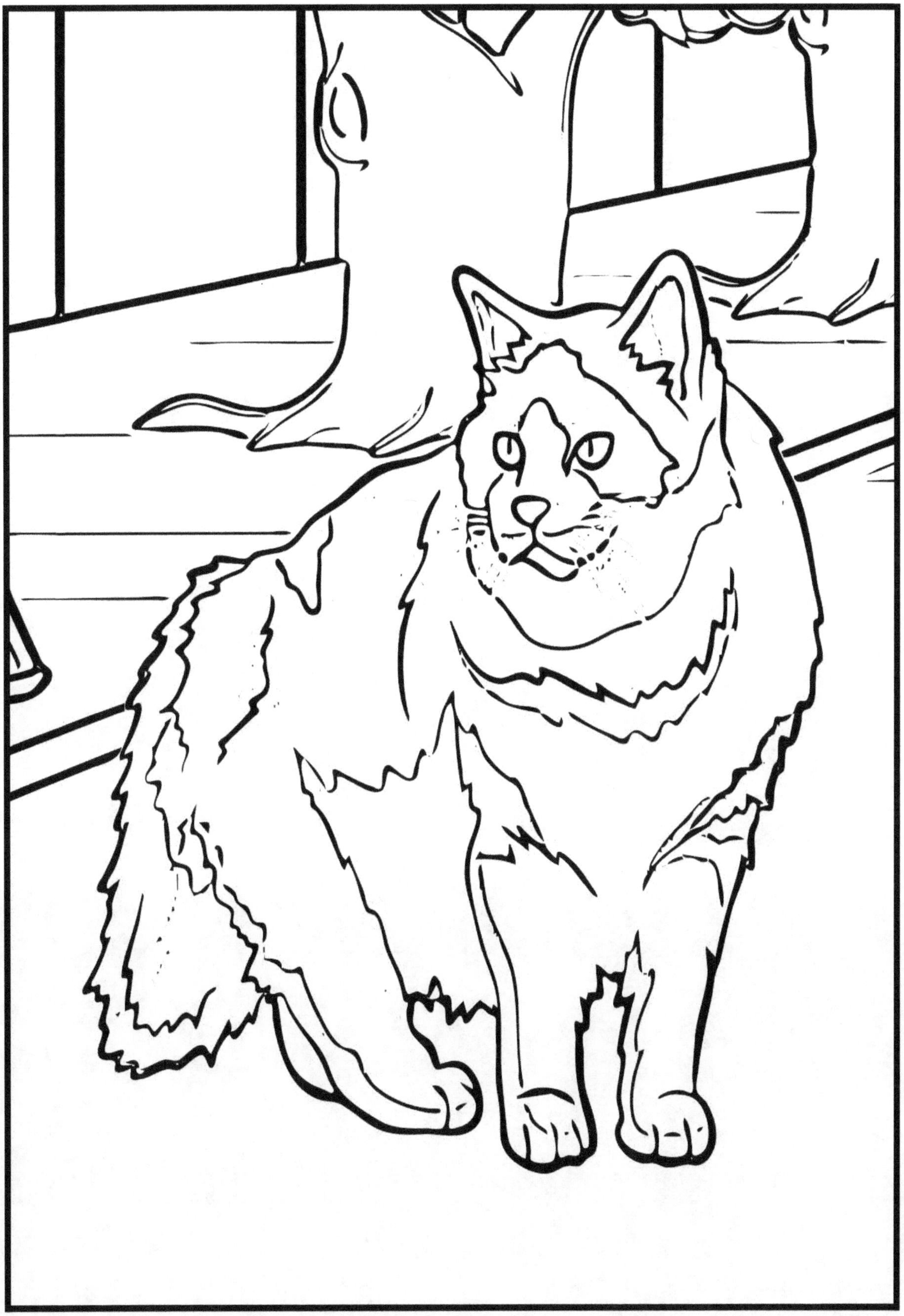

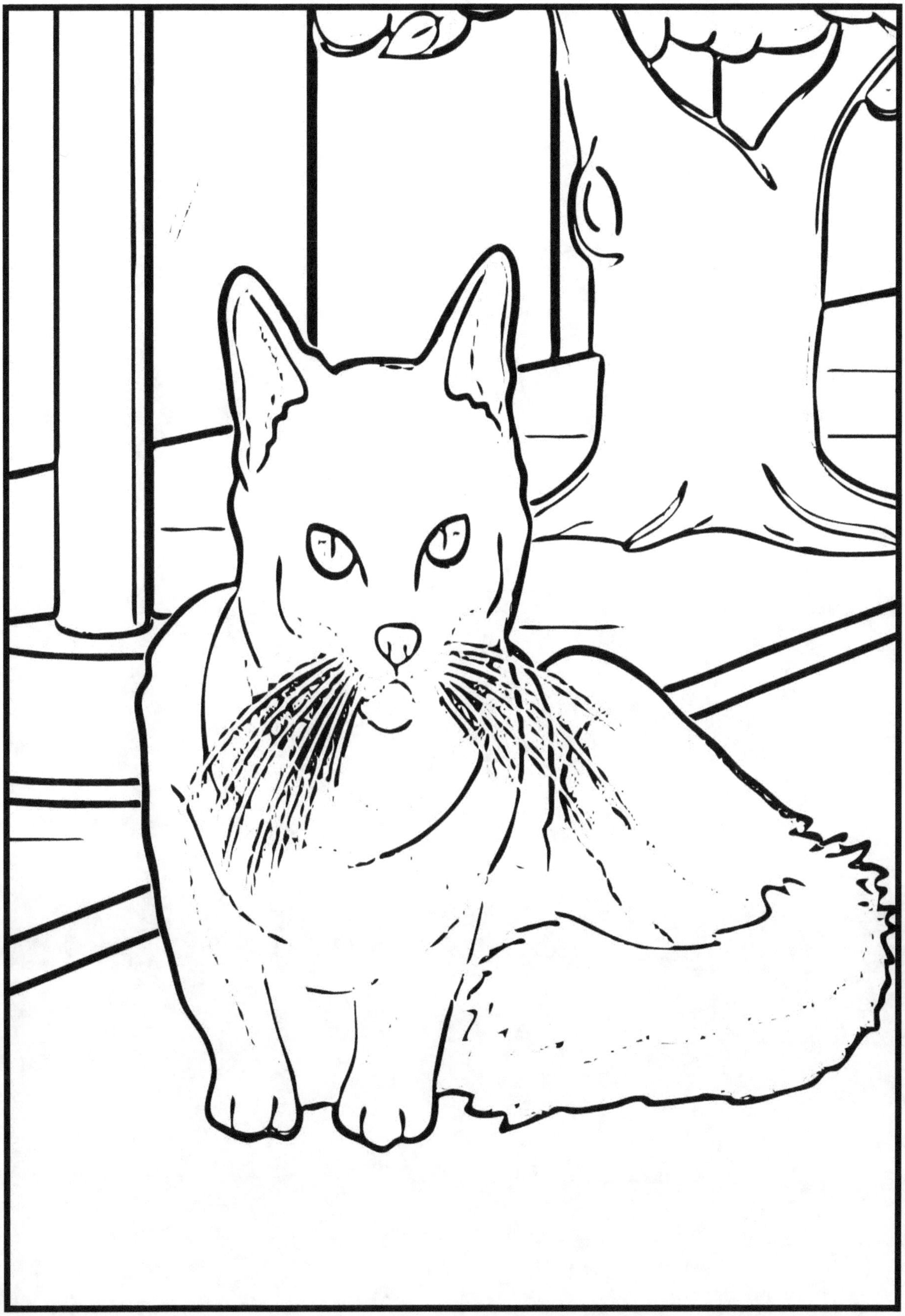

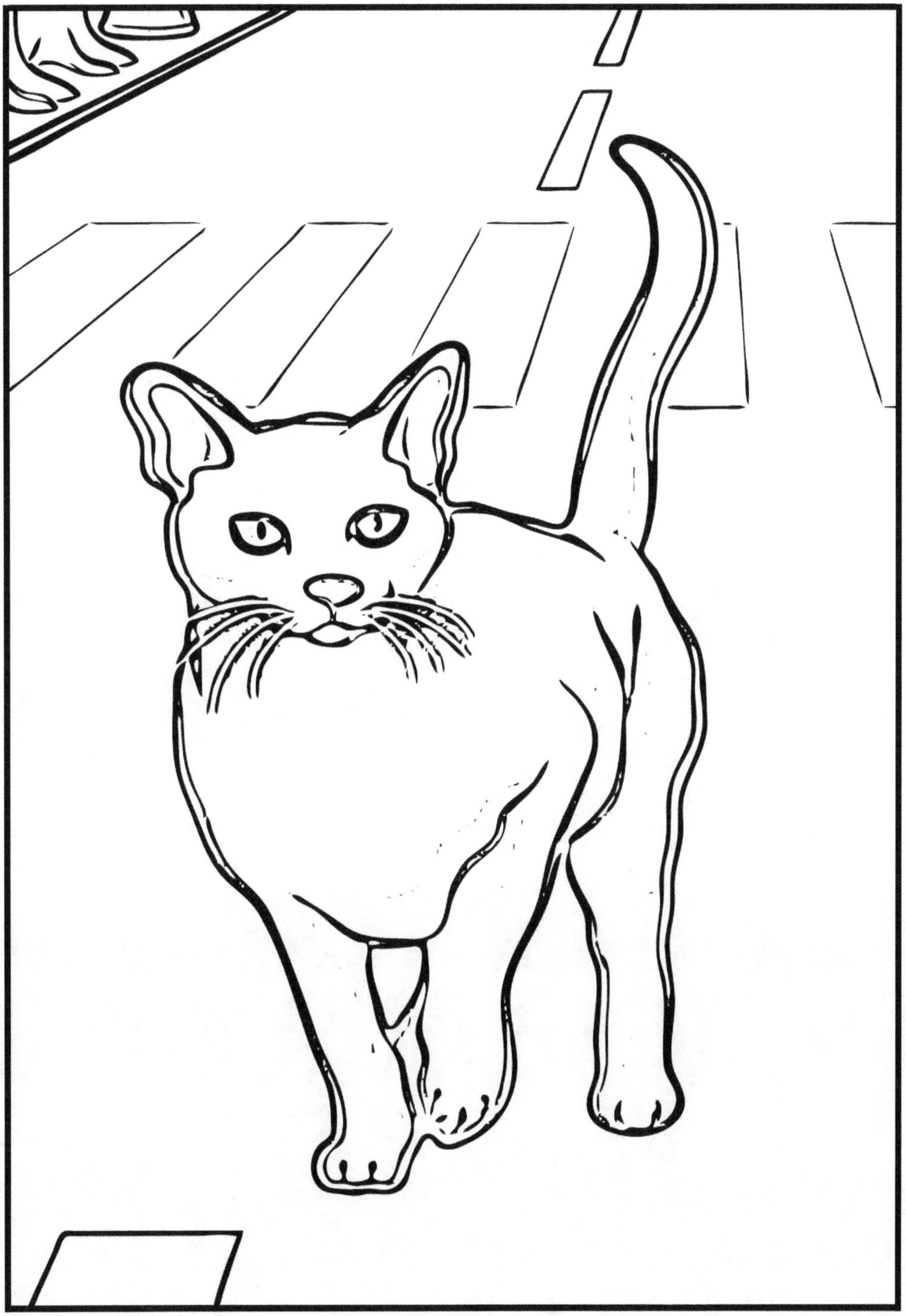

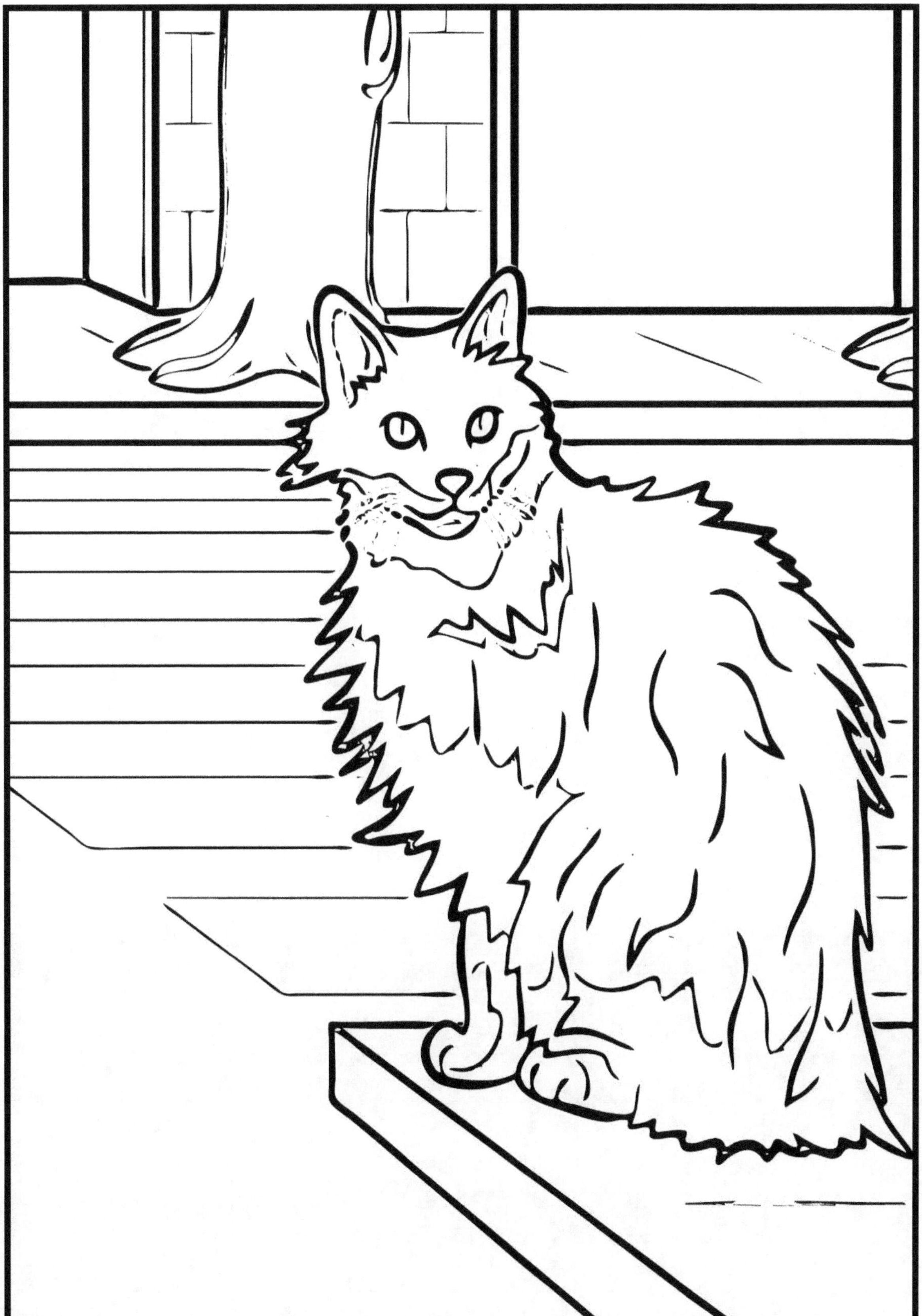

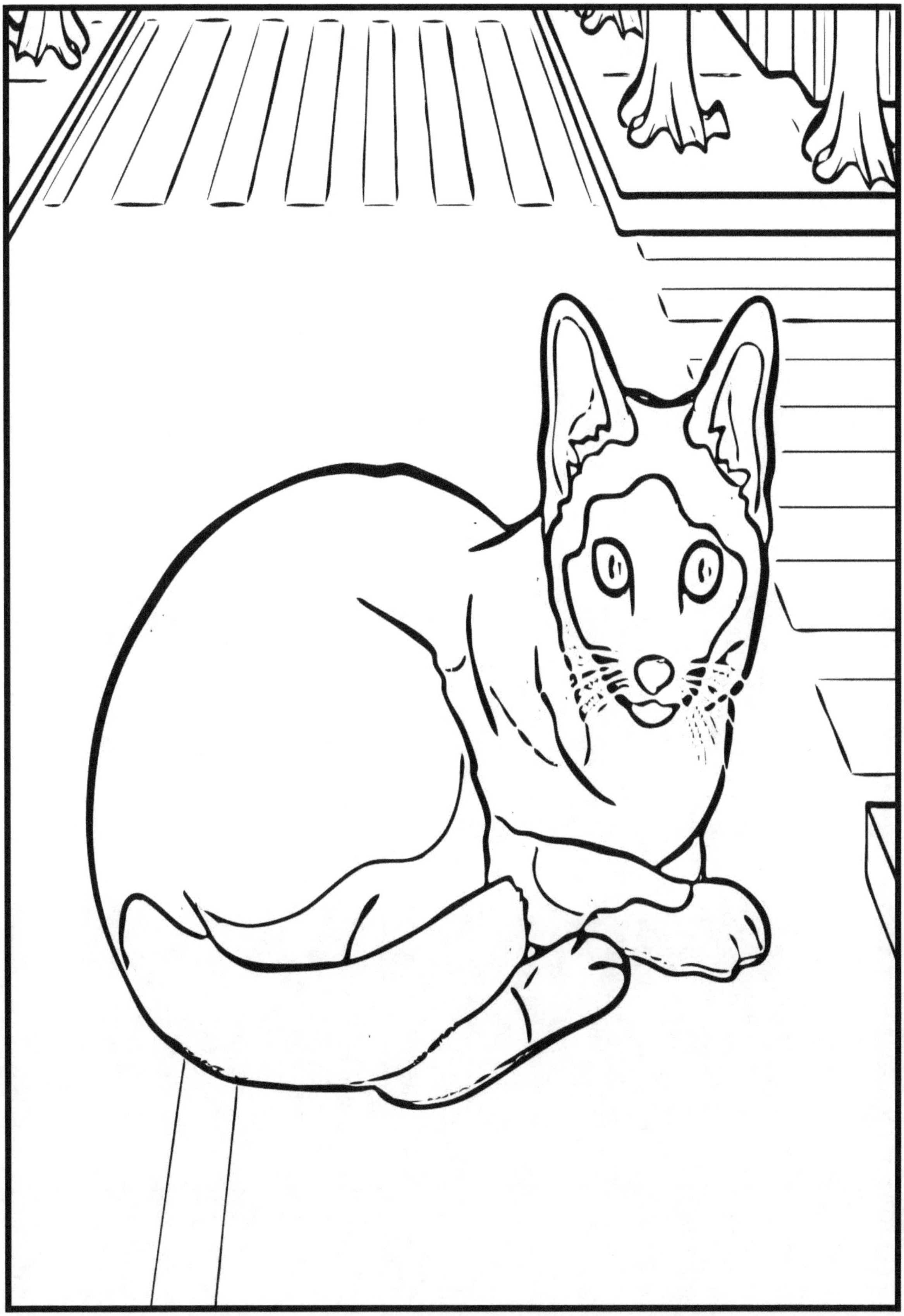

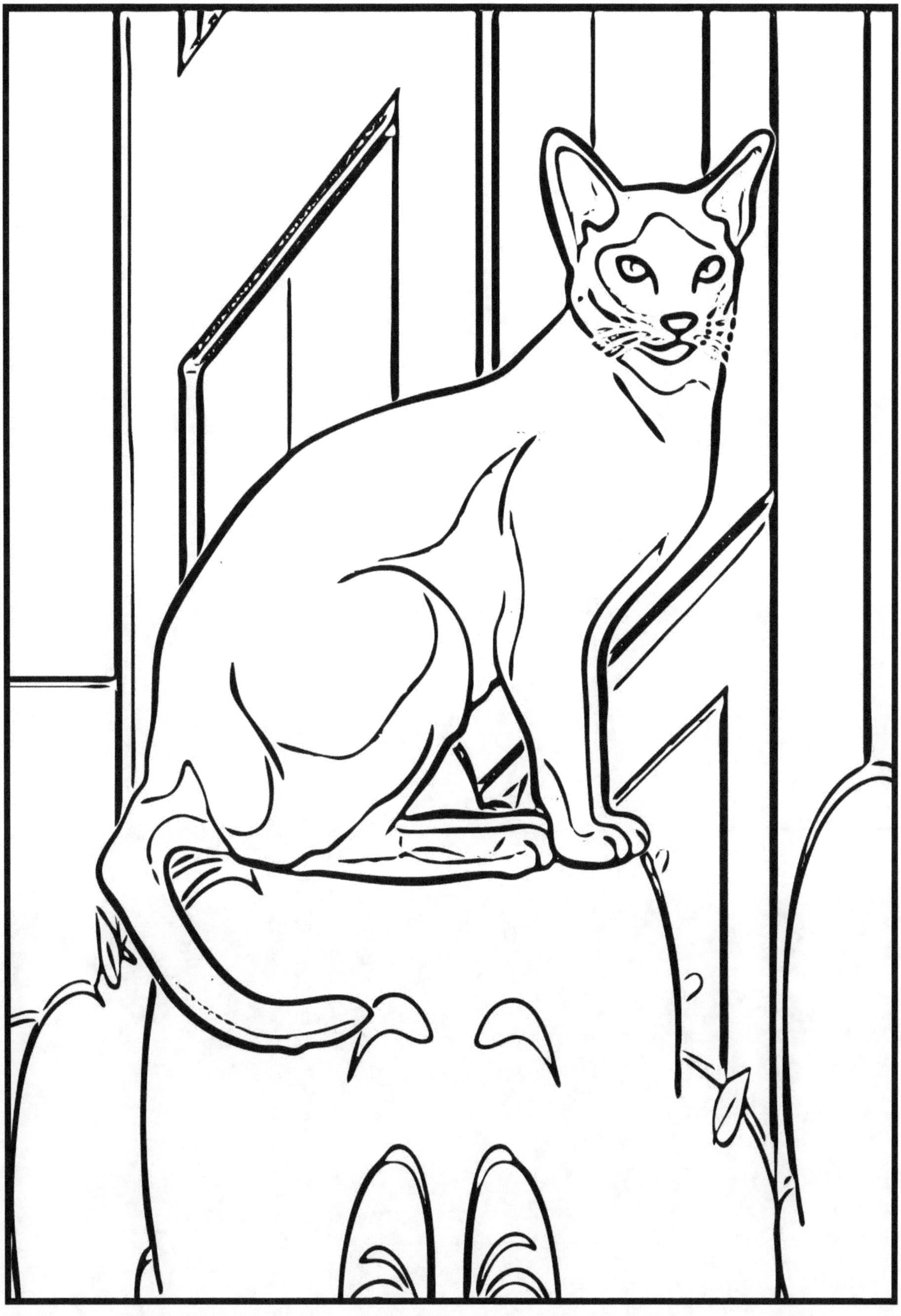

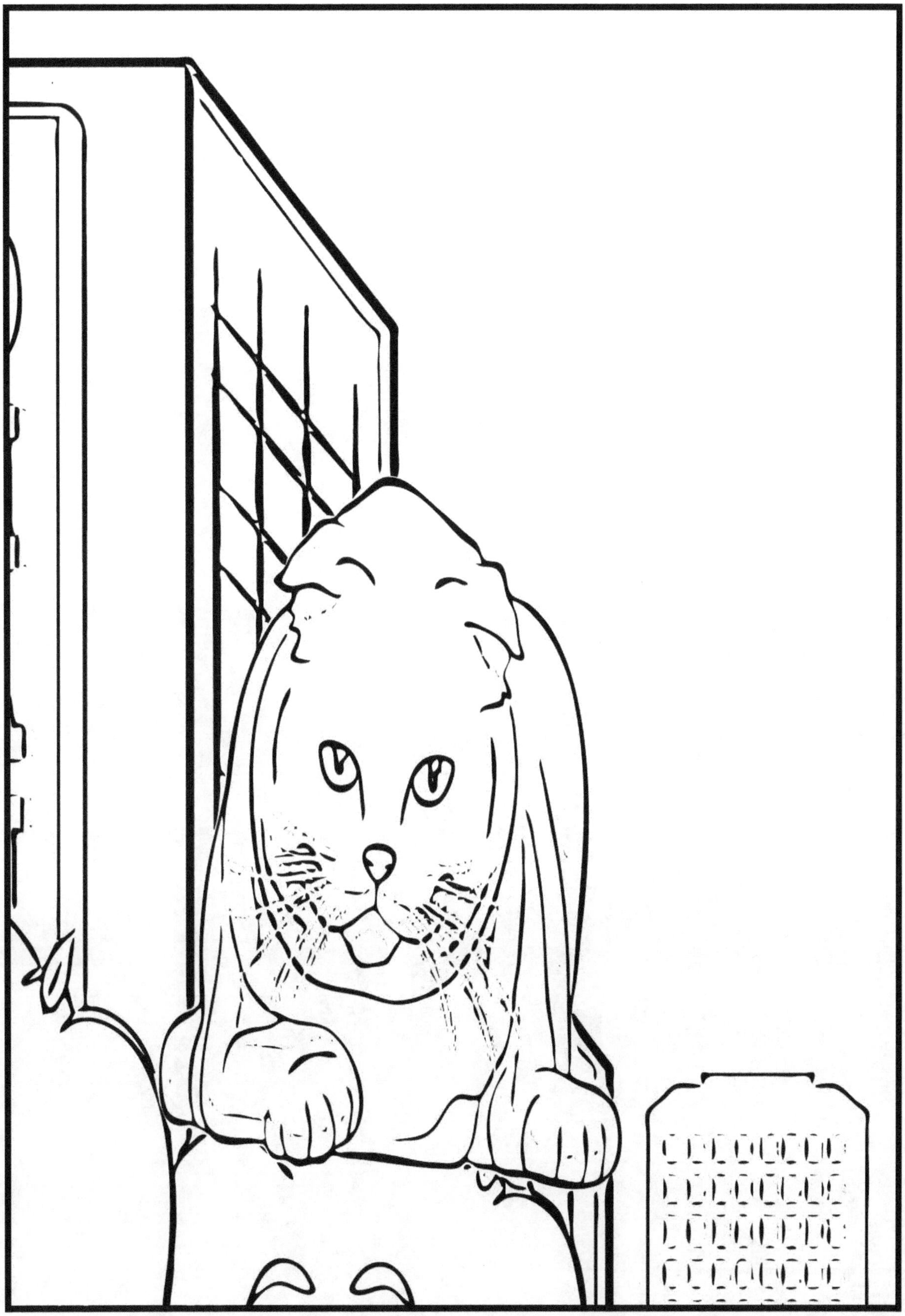

www.ingramcontent.com/pod-product-compliance
Lightning Source LLC
Chambersburg PA
CBHW080617180526
45168CB00007B/2955
* 9 7 8 1 5 1 9 1 8 9 4 5 5 *